Pocket Guide
to Stress

Pocket Guide to Stress

Richard Thompson
B.Sc. (Hons) Soc., PhD

Arlington Books
King Street, St. James's
London SW1

POCKET GUIDE TO STRESS
First published 1982
this new edition published 1987 by
Arlington Books (Publishers) Ltd
15-17 King Street, St. James's
London SW1

© *Richard Thompson 1982*

Typeset by Rapidset, London
Printed and bound by
Richard Clay Ltd, Suffolk

British Library Cataloguing in Publication Data

Thompson, Richard, 1946–
Pocket guide to stress.—2nd ed.
1. Stress (Psychology) 2. Stress
(Physiology)
I. Title
155.9   BF575.S75

ISBN 0–85140–713–7

Contents

About The Author

Dr Dick Thompson is a writer and broadcaster on topics of health and social concern, including stress and depression. He trained as a medical sociologist, receiving his doctorate in 1976. He is currently Director of the *Someone To Talk To* Project – a national database of self-help and community support agencies providing information and advice to professionals and to the general public. He is also Associate Director of the Mental Health Foundation and consultant to MPA Ltd, a development agency for charities and health care organisations.

Introduction

Think how often the word *stress* crops up in conversation or in magazine articles. It's almost as if we have discovered a new virus lurking in our homes and work places, waiting to pounce the moment our backs are turned. Yet stress is not generally thought of by doctors as an illness process – instead it tends to be regarded as a state in which people find themselves when they are subject to undue pressures and begin to show signs of strain and distress.

Paradoxically, family doctors treat cases of stress-related illness every day in their surgeries and surgeons quite often operate on people to remove diseased or malfunctioning organs that become unhealthy because of undiagnosed or unregulated stresses acting upon the body. It has been estimated, for example, that on top of the eight million consultations that GP's give each year for recognisable cases of mental illness, as many again are given for complaints of a stress-related nature.

Some recent research, funded by the Mental Health Foundation not only revealed that stress can produce symptoms of appendicitis, but also that out of 119 patients who had their appendixes removed 'nearly half had a healthy or relatively healthy appendix.' In fact, patients found to have healthy appendixes at the time of operation where *twice* as likely to have suffered from severe psychological stress caused by serious life-crises in the 9 months before their operations, than were genuine appendicitis patients.

Research on both sides of the Atlantic has shown that 'stressful life events' such as marital conflict, the death of someone dear to you, loss of a job, injury, moving home and taking on a mortgage, can all have an influence upon health. Events like these can actually predispose some people to illness ranging from minor ailments like the common cold and 'flu, through to serious disorders like heart disease. The problem with much of this research, however, is that it has proved difficult to explain why some people become ill while others do not, when faced by similarly stressful situations. One explanation could lie in our choice of words. 'Stress' is actually a natural state of readiness for action. When you say 'I enjoy working under stress' — there is no reason to suspect that you are not coping perfectly well. But when words like 'strain' and 'pressure' begin to crop up in conversation, the implication is that you are under too much stress and it is having a negative effect upon your performance and perhaps your health as well. For the purposes of this book, I shall distinguish between stress — the normal response to new demands, and strain — the abnormal response.

Strain is a major concern, because it occurs only when people have reached their limits and are failing to cope properly with fresh demands.

'Stress' is not an illness but 'strain' can lead to illness. Doctors know how to spot the tell-tale signs of strain, for example, when a patient complains of muzziness in the head, weakness, or aches and pains. We need to know what combinations of factors result in people failing to cope with pressures of various kinds and what can be done to avoid such pressures in the future. In this book, five sources of stress and strain are described — psychological, developmental, physical, environmental and social — each one, in its own way having an important influence on our lives. How such stresses can affect your health is discussed in the following sections and finally, to round off, some ways of helping yourself and for obtaining help are suggested.

1 Stress or Strain?

Most people prefer to think that they don't suffer from stress. After all, to admit to it is like saying you can't cope and this tends to carry with it associations of weakness and failure. This is probably why we are so good at convincing ourselves and those around us that things are fine, when actually, they are not.

'Stress' is a word that we reserve for a special response to everyday problems. You don't say, for example, 'a stress at work is giving me nightmares', you would use the word 'problem' because it comes more naturally. On the other hand you might say 'I've been under a lot of stress; — because these words convey a sense of pressure that you have been under.

One of the reasons why the word 'stress' is so vague, is because it is used to convey a number of different meanings. In its everyday usage, 'stress' refers to the experience of 'being under pressure' and carries with it the implication that you have a problem only when you fail to cope adequately with it.

The difficulty with this interpretation is that it fails to distinguish adequately between 'causes' and 'responses'. For example, the death of a relative may be the cause of stress, but the response to bereavement can also mean that you are under stress. It is for this reason that the word 'stressor' is reserved for those stress factors which impinge upon your life, whereas, the 'stress response', refers to the way in which you adapt to meet the challenge before you.

If this explanation seems unnecessarily complicated, then reflect, for a moment, on how the word 'stress' tends to be used. For a lot of people stress is thought of as the modern excuse for getting off work. In other words, there is nothing really wrong with you when you are 'under stress'. It is just self-indulgence. Then there is the achievement- motivated concept of stress which says that 'you never get anything done unless you are working under pressure'. People who take this attitude feel that stress is a *good* thing and that those who don't strive to achieve the maximum results at all times, are really lesser mortals.

A favourite stereotype is the stressed business executive who finds that the Law of Diminishing Returns begins to apply to his performance at work — the more effort he puts in, past a certain point, the smaller is the gain. He experiences frustration, yells at his secretary, makes decisions that he will later regret, works late every night and drives home like a maniac. Apart from the fact that this man will quite possibly experience tension headaches, stomach pain (perhaps even an ulcer) and insomnia, he might even succumb to a heart attack.

Although this business executive might seem to be a prime candidate for a stress Oscar, he is not alone in the running. We all, at some stage in the course of our lives, experience high levels of stress. But are we talking about stress here, or strain? This is an important point because it defines the difference between acceptable and unacceptable levels of stress in our lives. To use a simple analogy, the human organism is a bit like an iron bar in the sense that both can be put under stress until they reach the point where strain occurs and if the pressure continues to be applied, damage — even destruction — can follow.

It is to avoid the consequences of strain that careful attention is paid to potential stress factors in the building of a suspension bridge. By comparison we seem loathe to accord ourselves the same degree of respect, and yet, by failing to provide adequate safeguards against emotional and physical strain, we continually run the risk of over-stretching ourselves.

On top or on edge?

When you overload a car, you stand a good chance of damaging its suspension and once the damage is done, repair work becomes necessary. The human body reacts in much the same way to an over-load of stress. The curious thing about human beings however, is that they don't all react to stress in the same way. Despite physical weaknesses some people remain strong in the face of danger or threat, while others show signs of distress and inability to cope.

Of course, if you know that you can cope with the stresses that are about to be placed upon you, there is little chance of your experiencing distress of any kind. This is not the same thing as being subjected to sudden shocks. Although the chemical changes that take place within the body may appear similar in both cases, the psychological reaction will be different and it is this factor that largely determines how successfully an individual will adapt to the situation confronting him.

Highly motivated people often object to being told that 'stress' can have unwanted emotional and physical side-effects, because such people thrive on the feeling of being supercharged. When the adrenalin is pumping and all systems are 'go', you often feel as if you could take over the world. This is why so much creative work seems to derive from bursts of energy.

Depressed people, on the other hand, often feel unable to cope with even normal pressures and can fail to identify the reasons for their downswings of mood. Psychological disorders may have a strong stress-component because of the conflicting demands that are constantly being placed upon us. But it is the apparent susceptibility of certain people to strain that requires us to look more closely at the reasons why some people stay on top while others tend to go over the edge.

2 Sources of Stress and Strain

Nobody is free from stress. In fact without stress we would probably not survive as a species. As Dr. Malcolm Carruthers, one of Britain's leading authorities on the subject puts it:

'The human body and mind are built to take stress. In fact they thrive on it. An experiment with some athletes showed how the body deteriorates when all stress is taken off it. They were made to lie on their beds for a fortnight. Their muscles began to waste away, their bones began to soften and their internal organs and their blood systems functioned less well. This is one of the reasons why hospitals nowadays make patients get up as soon as possible after an operation. Although rest was once supposed to assist recovery, too much of it actually sets the body back.'

When referred to in this way, stress means stimulation and exertion and is seen as a normal part of healthy activity, but we all know how easy it is to over-extend or over-stimulate ourselves.

Too much drinking, too much physical exertion, too much mental pressure, in fact too much of anything can be bad for you and this is why we make the distinction between normal stress and strain or 'overstress'. The boundary between stress and strain is very tenuous and we often fail to recognise when we are going over the top.

Basically there are five major categories of stress, which, in excess, can have adverse effects upon peoples' lives. These are psychological stress, developmental stress, physical stress, environmental stress and social stress.

Psychological stress

Psychological stress doesn't mean 'mental disturbance' nor does it mean that you lose control of your senses. In fact, to be 'psychologically or emotionally stressed' can mean that you have a heightened awareness of the world around you and are functioning better than usual. But how can you tell if someone is experiencing psychological strain?

If you think about it, it's really not very difficult. People who appear anxious a lot of the time or are particularly aggressive for no apparent reason are probably struggling with some inner problem. Conversely, people who are unduly quiet and introspective, who shut themselves away or who seem withdrawn and listless may also be under stain.

Anxiety

In the case of anxiety, the stress or doesn't necessarily have to be real — like being given notice to quit your job — it may be imaginary and yet feel real enough. The point is that feelings of nervousness, tension, apprehension and fear are all unpleasant emotional sensations and they can set off exactly the same bodily reactions as actual threats.

Terror

Terror is an anxiety response that provokes massive changes in body chemistry. We know, for example, that the heart rate increases, blood pressure rises, breathing becomes faster and deeper, muscles tense and tighten and the pupils dilate — all part of the 'fight-flight' alarm reaction that we shall be discussing later.

You wouldn't normally expect to come across a terrified colleague at work, or, for that matter, a terrified member of your family when you get home. What you might find, on occasion, is someone who appears restless and nervous, whose hands tremble and whose facial expression seems taut and frightened. They might be breathing quickly, sweating lightly and complaining of 'flutters' in the chest, or, on the other hand be feeling unusually tired and lacking in energy.

No doubt, a little probing will lead you to discover the source of the problem, which will then enable you to take appropriate action. But would you have thought of this as a case of psychological strain, or would you have put it down to something more tangible like 'overtiredness', or some other situational factor?

We know how to identify anxiety because it is usually visible in peoples' expressions and actions. What we may not understand are the reasons why, at certain times, strain occurs. This raises the question of whether some people are anxiety-prone or have anxious personalities.

It is difficult to talk of hereditary anxiety, but there is no doubt that anxiety can run in families. Anxious parents can breed anxious children, not in the genetic sense, but through the atmosphere or environment of the home. When faced by a challenge in later life, the insecurity experienced as a child might sway the balance between succeeding or failing, coping and not coping.

Thus, a person who is offered promotion and suddenly finds himself feeling panicky, even physically sick at the thought of new responsibilities, quickly reaches his stress threshold (see *Figure 1*) and, depending upon such factors as strength of personality and support from others around him, either copes with the stress or begins to experience distress.

Minor illnesses commonly result from strain and quite often, psychological distress is evident. Very occasionally prolonged over-stress due to anxiety will result in severe physical or mental illness and it is not uncommon for past traumas to manifest themselves in the form of illness at some later date.

Phobias

Phobias of various kinds may be the result of unresolved anxieties and they can have dramatic effects. Claustrophobia, the fear of being enclosed in confined spaces, is a particularly stressful condition for those who, for example, have to travel by Underground or who use lifts regularly. The psychological fear of being swallowed-up or suffocated may bring

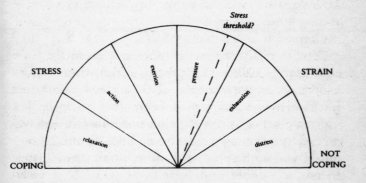

Fig. 1   Stress and over-arousal.

on an attack of asthma, cause palpitations, create

a feeling of light-headedness and nausea and even prompt an hysterical outburst of screaming and crying. Later, as the body's metabolism begins to return to normal, residual side-effects such as blotches on the skin, diarrhoea and pins and needles may occur.

Agoraphobia, or the fear of open spaces, similarly affects people in distressing ways.

Pathological Types
People differ markedly in the way in which they handle stress. Outward going, aggressive types seem to have all the confidence in the world until some seemingly minor event upsets them. All along, they may have been hiding an insecurity about succeeding. Being aggressive means that you generate your own stresses, because of the opposition you create amongst others.

Competitive people, similarly, find that they make life difficult for themselves because they are constantly challenging others. Competition goes hand in hand with success or failure and this means learning how to cope with both. It is not true that success always brings happiness, because it depends on how you achieved success and how much it took out of you in the process. Failure, on the other hand, breeds self-doubt and insecurity, which can mean attempting to block-out the misery through alcohol, drugs and other methods of tranquillisation.

As society becomes more competitive and the pressure to succeed continues to grow, we should perhaps not be surprised that levels of stress-related illness are on the increase. While the media continue to encourage people to indulge themselves in so-called stress-reducing behaviour like drinking and smoking, the results can only speak for themselves.

Quiet types, may at first sight, seem like perfectly adjusted human beings who never suffer a day's strain in their lives. But lurking behind that wall of silence can be a sensitive individual who can't cope too well with the noisy, pressurising, aggressive types referred to above. It is important to know whether a friend, colleague or member of the family is quiet because that is their nature or because they are actually unhappy or distressed.

Depression, unlike anxiety, is characterised by a lowering of mood and can have quite serious consequences if not properly diagnosed or treated early enough. Stress can play an important role, particularly if the individual concerned already has a low stress threshold.

Developmental stress

Developmental stress refers to the process of growth and maturation and concerns adaptation to change throughout life. Since the theme of this book is how the individual learns to select appropriate and effective ways of dealing with stress and strain, the subject of growth, development and ageing is particularly important. Whether we care to accept it or not, we cannot ignore the fact that from our first days on this earth we are subjected to numerous and often conflicting demands from our fellow citizens. Right from the beginning, we have the task of learning how to adapt to other peoples' expectations of ourselves.

If all things were equal, this might not be such a difficult task, but human nature being what it is, often makes it hard for us to get back what we put into the 'system'. The frustrations and the failures that we experience throughout life reflect our ability to live up to what we expect of ourselves and of others, which explains why coping with stress has a lot to do with coping with people.

Childhood

Children are not given the choice of deciding whether they wish to be born but they are nevertheless expected to conform to the standards set by the society into which they emerge. Before the age of three, young children are particularly susceptible to outside influences and any emotional deprivation or confusion at this stage can affect personality growth.

Babies and very young children who are separated from their mothers or who are denied affection when they most need it, may become withdrawn and show signs of insecurity as they grow older. Quite possibly, as adults, they may find giving and receiving love to be difficult, which will influence how they make relationships. The stresses that they experience will be magnified each time a relationship goes wrong, compounding the sense of insecurity and inadequacy that they already feel. Because of their low stress threshold, emotional strain may become evident as coping becomes more of a problem.

School undoubtedly provides the first real test of a child's ability to cope with the world. It is here that children first learn to identify with a whole range of new people. Schooldays are not always the best days of childrens' lives. Difficulties in making friends and learning to cope with competition are common and probably account for much of the misery and unhappiness that is sometimes experienced at this stage.

An anxious or depressed child may exhibit distress either through aggressive behaviour and hyperactivity or withdrawal and listlessness. Because young children are not always able to communicate their feelings, we need to be constantly aware of behavioural changes.

Older children, when they get into the middle-school years, have usually started to think for themselves and to act independently which is when they first find themselves vulnerable to failure and criticism. They start kicking at the traces and ignoring advice from adults, only to discover that the advice was probably correct in the first place.

Unfortunately, the lessons learned during this stage of development can be quite painful both in terms of personality growth and achievement. Over-stress can occur which a child's illusions are shattered and he sees his dreams evaporating in front of his eyes.

Perhaps this is what growing-up is all about and why support needs to be provided for those who find it difficult to cope from time to time.

Adolescents probably have one of the toughest deals that life can offer. They are expected to behave like adults, yet are often still treated like children. This conflict can prove particularly stressful to some young people, because it happens at a time when all kinds of new and complex physical changes are also taking place. If adolescents are quiet, they are labelled as 'moody'. If they are exuberant, they are being 'immature'. Depression is often mistaken for self-indulgence and expressions of opinion as 'arrogance'. When teenagers complain about being misunderstood, they are not just making a statement about their independence from the adult world. They might actually be experiencing deep personal conflict and yet find it difficult to convey their feelings of anxiety, inadequacy or loneliness. For this reason, no young person should be patronised or ignored when they appear to be in distress, even if it has all happened before.

Apart from the physical changes, adolescents have to cope with changes in their status and identity. At 16 they can ride motorbikes and leave school. Girls can have a legal abortion without parental consent. Voting rights become mandatory at the age of 18. The kinds of decisions that are made throughout the teenage years increase in significance, reflecting the emergence of responsibility. Whether at the age of 18 young people are able to assume adult responsibilities will depend to a large extent on how well they have coped with the process of adaptation from childhood to young adulthood.

Adulthood

The late teens and early twenties is, generally, the time when decisions have to be made. Passing exams, finding a job, going to University, are all major events which carry their own stresses and affect people in different ways. Every decision becomes a responsibility and, consequently, every mistake a problem.

Motherhood

You wouldn't normally think having a baby could be the cause of emotional distress, but for some women it can mean months of misery. All kinds of changes in status take place during pregnancy and to add to her new awareness of the physical changes taking place, the mother-to-be has to consider what to do about her job (if she is working) and how to continue with existing responsibilites in the home.

Post-natal depression occurs in about one in ten women and can last up to six months. Although hormonal changes do play an important part in this condition, there is no doubt that the process of adaptation is a stress.

It should not be forgotten that women are under considerable pressure to achieve what is expected of them over a shorter time span than that allotted to men. There is a kind of mythology which states that a girl should find a husband before she is on the shelf and have a baby before it is too late. This all adds up to pressure, subtle though it may be and it is because of these imposed arbitrary time limits that stress and strain become a feature of development.

Middle Age

The 'mid-life crisis' is one of those phrases that describes the 'last fling of youth' as if, at around 45, old age begins to descent and youth slips away beyond our grasp! Just like the mythology that surrounds a woman's supposed fight to stay young, the so-called crisis of middle age is equally misleading. Middle age is a time of re-evaluation. Where young adults have to cope with all the pressures of establishing themselves in the world, adults reaching middle age have to face the possibility that they have not achieved what they wanted when they were younger. In this sense failure to live up to expectations is an important stress factor in development.

Physical changes take on a greater significance at this stage in life because they are associated with ageing rather than maturing. For woman this process tends to assume added importance because they come to the end of their childbearing years and during their late forties and early fifties experience the menopause.

Men have to contend with increasing risks of illness particularly when a sedentary life-style replaces a previously active and health-conscious way of life. The incidence of heart disease, for example, reaches a peak for men in their forties and stress has been identified as one of the major causes along with smoking, rich diet and high blood pressure.

The loss of physical attraction for one's partner is not uncommon in middle age and if reassurance is not forthcoming, attention may be turned to someone else who can provide it. Marriages come under strain at this stage in life because things that were taken for granted are questioned for the first time.

Having painted a rather negative picture of middle age, it should be remembered that for the majority of people, this is still the time when most is achieved. Stress is a normal part of this process and the occasional distress experienced acts as a reminder that change is not always smooth.

Retirement and Beyond

Growing old for most people causes few problems of adaptation. With the average life expectancy approaching eighty, however, we need to take account of all the limitations that old people experience as their faculties begin to decline and their mobility becomes restricted.

Not all elderly people experience distress in later life, but those who do often have good reason. Physical problems due to lack of fitness, illness or disease can make life quite unbearable, particularly if pain restricts movement or deterioration of mental faculties occurs. Social changes that follow in the wake of retirement can be difficult to accept. Loss of income, loss of status, endless free time and moving to a new environment can be very stressful particularly for people who have been used to active work and social life.

Isolation becomes a problem the older you get. If a partner dies and the family are not in the immediate vicinity, it's easy to feel isolated and to develop a negative attitude towards life. Depression is common amongst old people, especially if they begin to feel useless and helpless. They may appear to be 'losing their grip' by failing to remember things or when speech becomes impaired, but this is not necessarily a sign of early senility.

The problem with old age is that people lose their adaptability and become subject to strain more easily than in earlier years. As the stress threshold is reached more often, distress becomes a more regular occurrence. Of course, it is quite possible that under-stress is to blame for some elderly peoples' problems of adaptation, because of the lack of stimulation they receive. Failure to cope can arise as easily from neglect and isolation as from physical pain and over-exertion.

Physical stress

Physical stress refers to the effects of over-exertion as well as to bodily changes that affect mood, which can be the result of illness, biochemical imbalances, drugs, alcohol, dietary problems and allergies.

Activity and Strain
When you see footballers limping off a pitch or athletes doubling up in pain on the track, you generally think of them as having strained a muscle or a tendon. What has happened is that too much pressure has been exerted on a particular part of the body, with the result that damage has occured and movement is subsequently restricted.

As our bodies regulate the amount of energy that we use up in activity, we maintain a balance between under-stimulation and over-tiredness. There are times, however, when we, quite simply, over-do things, with the result that some part of the body gives up under the strain and we experience pain or discomfort. The difference between 'stress' and 'strain', as we have already seen, lies in our ability to adapt to new demands that are placed upon us. In this sense, 'physical stress' refers to the body's response to pressure, whereas 'physical strain' refers to its inability to cope with that pressure.

Illness and Injury
Any kind of illness or injury places the body under stress. We all know what it's like to be in bed with 'flu, when your head aches, your muscles feel like lead and thinking becomes an effort. Depending upon how fit you were previously, the amount of time it

takes to recover will vary. Furthermore, the longer the illness the longer the period of recuperation will be.

Weakness is a common after-effect of illness or injury. The body has to fight hard to protect itself from further damage and, in the process of eliminating viruses or repairing damaged tissue, considerable amounts of energy are used up. Minor illnesses or injuries rarely strain the body and providing that sensible action is taken from the outset, there is no reason to fear that recovery will be delayed.

The mind-body link in illness and disease processes has always fascinated doctors. 'Psychosomatic illness' (*psyche* — mind, *soma* — body) tends to be either in or out of fashion. However, there is growing evidence that some physical disorders are stress-related, particularly with respect to severe emotional trauma. The theory here is that a major shock can stun the body's immune system, allowing viruses to roam freely and 'rogue cells' to develop unchecked by the body's normal defences.

Pain is both a physical source of distress as well as being psychologically debilitating. If relief is not forthcoming the strain can be immense and some people literally lose their will to live when pain becomes intolerable.

Old age can be particularly stressful both from a physical and psychological point of view. As bodily functions deteriorate, distress increases. Failing memory, slurred speech, impaired sight and hearing, incontinence — are all very difficult to cope with and they can be equally stressful for caring relatives. Any kind of personal handicap, whether it be physical or mental, can cause distress. Adapting to a world organised and run by able-bodied people can be difficult to come to terms with both physically and psychologically. Even when temporary in-capacitation results in periods off work, or spells in hospital, the business of adapting to the change can prove difficult for all concerned.

Hormonal and biochemical factors

The body continually releases hormones into the bloodstream in response to internal and external stimuli and sometimes too many or too few are present, result in an alteration of mood. Thyroid problems, for example, are well known for causing overactivity or depression.

Women experience numerous hormonal changes during the menstrual cycle, childbirth and the meno-pause. Pre-menstrual tension, pre and post-natal depression and menopausal depression are common reactions to changes in hormone balances. The 'ups' and 'downs' associated with these conditions can range from mild anxiety or irritability to aggressive-ness and tearfulness followed by withdrawal.

In psychiatry, the term 'endogenous' is used to describe disorders which 'come from within', having no obvious external cause. Depression, for example, may be triggered off by a physical illness, a change in hormone balance, even by certain drugs, although that cause may not be evident. One of the difficulties that people face when they are depressed in this way is that they cannot explain how this situation came about, which adds an additional stress to an already distressing condition. People who suffer from manic depression experience 'cyclothymic' mood swings, ranging from hypomania, when they sleep less and appear to have boundless, sometimes uncontrollable energy, to deep depression — often accompanied by suicidal feelings. It is a depressive condition that gives cause for alarm because of the risk of suicide that exists when the person reaches rock bottom.

Alcohol and Drugs

Alcohol may make you feel good for a while, but it will slow your responses, distort your perception and finally, put you to sleep. Alcohol, in fact, depresses rather than activates the metabolism, which is why a single drink seems to have more potency when you are already tired. The incidence of alcoholism in the UK is on the increase and there is little doubt that drinking, even as a social habit, is used to relieve stress. The trouble with drinking for this reason is that while problems disappear for the time being, they are still there the next day — when you may not be in the best shape to deal with them.

People take drugs, legally and illegally, for much the same reason that they consume alcohol. Drink and drugs may well provide temporary relief, even stimulation, but in excess they cause rather than solve problems. Although we talk about heroin addiction as if it was the only example of drug abuse, we should also consider the degree of dependence that the average person has upon alcohol, aspirin and valium, for these readily-available potions are now marketed as standard ways of relieving the stresses of everyday life.

Dietary factors
The food we eat is important to health and well-being especially when much of what we consume is highly refined and often lacking in essential nutrients and vitamins. Furthermore, because we are subject to greater pressure due to the pace of modern life, we need the right balance of essential ingredients in food, to maintain our energy levels. Poor nutrition results in depleted energy and a lowered resistance to infection.

Environmental stress

Overcrowding and anti-social behaviour in cities
City life is stressful by virtue of the sheer volume of people having to live within confined spaces. When a combination of factors such as poor housing, unemployment and social deprivation occur together, the strain of living displays itself in vandalism, crime, poor mental and physical health and suicide. The fact that people survive such conditions does not mean

that they can adapt indefinitely. Anti-social acts such as muggings, burglary and riots are an expression of strain in a city environment.

At a more local level, overcrowding in homes or offices can also produce tensions and strain. Overcrowded offices are notorious for causing rows and inefficiency as it becomes impossible to concentrate with the noise of telephones, typewriters and talking taking place around you.

Sensory stress

Noise has been recognised as a major sensory stress for some years. Uncontrollable noise lowers peoples' stress and thresholds by decreasing their tolerance to frustration and making them prone to aggressive outbursts. Over long periods, persistent noise can increase anxiety levels leaving people prone to ailments such as headaches, migraine and hypertension, and to accidents.

Very little importance has been attached to sources of light as potential stressors, but recent research point convincingly in this direction. Daylight has a clearly definable organising role in body functions and its absence can result in physical and psychological stress reactions.

Media stress

Television and the media contribute to stress by depicting life in a way that is often unobtainable for the average viewer. Advertising seduces people into believing that they should strive to obtain a lifestyle that will be admired by others. In reality, most people cannot afford to purchase the luxury items that are presented to them on television or in magazines. It is easy to understand how, under the circumstances, people get depressed and suffer feelings of failure when things don't match up to their expectations.

Of course, the media has educational functions as well and we would certainly be far less well-informed without them. But we may need to strike more of a balance between what we need and what we are told we should have.

Social stress

We are essentially social animals but the trouble with co-existing with our fellow man is that they don't always live up to our expectations and quite often this leads to conflict. 'Social stress' is, if you like, the normal state of affairs that exists in a society where each member learns to weigh-up conflicting demands and expectations and to act accordingly. 'Social strain' is when something goes wrong in the course of our interactions with others and coping becomes a problem.

There are definite pressures that society places upon us from a very early age, we are taught to obey rules and to adhere to codes of conduct that determine our acceptability in the eyes of others. Society has its own rules and if they are ignored the pressure to conform is great. This probably explains why adolescence is punctuated by periods of anxiety and clashes with authority.

These more general social processes influence an individual's ability to adapt to the demands of society and naturally, there will be occasions when these demands are too great and strain is experienced. Riots may well be a collective manifestation of social strain — and war, the expression of conflict between people when the aim is to cause rather than alleviate distress.

Interpersonal Stress
When we talk about 'marital stress' or 'work stress', we are saying something about the quality of our experience in marriage or at work. Not suprisingly, problems develop from time to time due to pressures or conflicts that arise between people. Unresolved resentment for example can smoulder as a stress for years in an unhappy marriage. Strained relationships occur in all walks of life and can result in protracted arguments, dislike of peoples' company or even a desire for complete separation. Marriages under strain often end in divorce; sexual relationships can go wrong and result in anxiety and loss of interest; relationships with colleagues at work can become strained for all kinds of reasons and produce resentment.

Relationships with the opposite sex can be harmonious or fraught with problems. Conflicting interests, competitive jobs, adherence to traditional views about the male or female 'role', sexual incompatibility, anti-social habits and insensitivity — are just some of the issues that can put strain on a relationship.

Women in many respects today, face more stress than they have previously. There is less protection now than there was in the traditional male/female relationship, when the man assumed overall authority. A woman can now expect to have a career, an income equal to that of a man, a free social and sexual life and the right to determine the course of her life both within marriage and outside it. However, much of this freedom can be illusory, particularly if a woman still has to run a home, look after her husband and care for her children — on top of her job. Resentment is to be expected in a situation like this, because in reality a woman not only has to cope with new, but all the traditional responsibilities as well.

Sexual problems
These occur for a variety of reasons. Loss of attraction can be the result of taking a partner for granted or simply forgetting that he or she needs reassurance and affection. Pressure at work and rush hour commuting, are just some of the factors that can reduce one's interest in sex and the attraction of one's partner. Being sexually demanding at inappropriate times can result in rejection and accusations of

insensitivity. When these disagreements become conflicts, strain occurs and relationships can deteriorate.

Stress at work
This may be due to the nature of the work
environment — as in the case of assembly-line or
repetitive jobs, but it can also arise from too much
pressure, too little consideration by others and simple
disagreements with colleagues. A difficult boss can
make life hell for a conscientious employee who
can't say 'no' to more work. A competitive colleague
may get all the praise for work that you initiated
and a secretary can put potential clients off by an

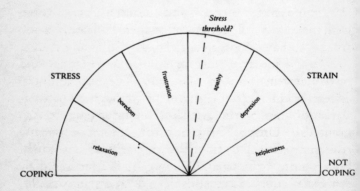

Fig. 2.   Stress and under-arousal

over-casual telephone manner. When it is you that carries responsibilities for what people do, such problems can easily built up and lead to strain.

As a measure of how people fail to cope with work stress, time off work with stress related illnesses is estimated to have increased by 500% since the mid 1950's.

Not all jobs are stressful because they over-stretch people. Boring, dull, repetitive jobs can be equally stressful because they fail to motivate the employee with the result that he or she feels underused and lethargic. Frustration quickly builds up when you cannot see initiative and expend your energy constructively. (see *Figure 2*)

Redundancy and unemployment
Unemployment becomes a health hazard when inactivity and frustration are present. To have a job means to have status in society, as well as an income. To lose a job is to lose one's income, identity and credibility in the eyes of others. The psychological effect of unemployment can be damaging, particularly for someone whose skills are not being used in any way. Unless activities can be found to occupy the mind as well as the body, lethargy creeps in and a sense of hopelessness takes over. Worry about financial matters causes considerable strain on a family, especially if severe cut-backs have to be made. Some people turn to drink just to help them get through the

Social Readjustment Rating Scale

Event	Life Crises Unit Score	Own Score
Death of wife or husband	100	
Divorce	73	
Marital separation	65	
Jail term	63	
Death of close family member	63	
Personal injury or illness	53	
Marriage	50	
Getting the sack from work	47	
Marital reconciliation	45	
Retirement	45	
Change in health of family member	44	
Pregnancy	40	
Sexual problems	39	
Addition of new family member	39	
Major business problems	39	
Change in financial state	38	
Death of a close friend	37	
Change to different kind of work	36	
Change in living arrangements with wife/husband	35	
Taking on a large mortgage	31	
Foreclosure of mortgage or loan	30	
Change in responsibilities at work	29	
Son or daughter leaving home	29	
Trouble with in-laws	29	

Social Readjustment Rating Scale

Event	Life Crises Unit Score	Own Score
Outstanding personal achievement	28	
Wife starts/stops work	26	
Starting or leaving school	26	
Change in living conditions	25	
Revision of personal habits	24	
Trouble with the boss	23	
Change in working hours or conditions	20	
Change in residence	20	
Change in school	20	
Change in recreation	19	
Change in church activities	19	
Change in social activity	18	
Taking on a bank loan or HP debt	17	
Change in sleeping habits	16	
Change in number of family reunions	15	
Change in eating habits	16	
Vacation	13	
Christmas	12	
Minor violations of the law	11	

day and it is not unknown for cumulative pressure to result in suicide.

It is hard to calculate the long-term results of unemployment, but researchers in the USA have linked it with rising levels of baby battering, infant deaths due to under-feeding and suicide. It has even been suggested that a one per cent rise in the jobless total above an unemployment level of 9%, was directly responsible for 37,000 additional deaths due to compensatory over-drinking and heart disease. In this country, however, no accurate figures have been collected to substantiate such claims.

Life-crisis and illness

We have seen how interpersonal and work stresses can cause problems of coping and it has been suggested that strain can result in ill-health if it is not dealt with early enough. What we shall now do is to look at how life-crisis can affect health.

Two American doctors Thomas Holmes and Richard Rahe constructed what they refer to as a *Social Readjustment Rating Scale* which scores life-events on a serious to least serious basis. The scoring method was arrived at after exhaustive interviews and the scale you see on the following pages is a series of scores that reflect the average person's assessment of difficulty in adjusting to life-event changes.

If you would like to assess your own 'life-stress score', rate the forty-three items on the Rating Scale by filling in the blank spaces beneath the heading 'Own Score'. You are asked to consider 'marriage' as the mean, to which, in this case, we will give a score of 50. When you read each of the other life-event descriptions, ask yourself whether they would require a greater or lesser degree of adjustment and assign a score accordingly. If some of the descriptions do not apply to you, then (providing you are being honest with yourself) ignore them. When you have reached the end, add up your total and then read on.

Magnitude of life crisis	*Score*
Mild	150–199
Moderate	200–299
Severe	300

In the study, 37% of life-crisis that were scored between 150 and 199, were associated with a health change, this association rose to 51% with scores between 200 and 299, and to 79% with scores of 300 and above. In other words, the greater the stress, the more likely you are to experience ill-health.

If you happen to have a score in excess of 199, don't panic. Remember, the life-events scale is designed to be a guide to recent life experiences and should be used in association with a medical check-up. If your score is high, for example, if you have lost a loved-one recently, or if you have experienced a series

How Stress Affects Your Health

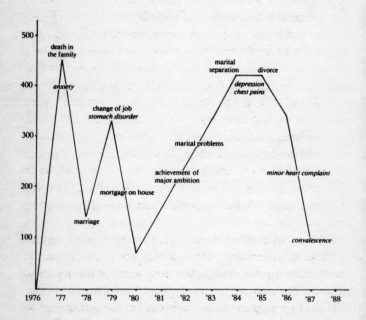

Fig. 3 A typical range of life-stress events over a period of 11 years with resultant illnesses and physical complaints. Assume that the person who has charted the Life Crisis Unit scores is male, aged 32 in 1976.

of unfortunate set backs, then you should be aware that such events can influence the overall pattern of your health.

There is a theory that the difference in susceptibility to illness consequent upon stressful life-events, can be explained in terms of personality. The idea is that there are two types of people — A's and B's — who run their lives in quite different ways. The type A person suffers from the 'hurry-worry syndrome', while the type B, is more realistic about what can and can't be achieved and tends to take life at a more even pace. A's are those people who succumb more easily to stress diseases. They move quickly, talk fast and emphatically, expect a lot from other people and despite their own belief that they are 'easy to get along with', they are probably the most awkward customers to deal with. On the other hand, they are efficient, have a lot of drive and can be highly creative and innovative.

B's, on the other hand, are not necessarily quiet or lacking in energy, it's just that they don't see the point in being forceful when they can get things done by quiet persuasion or the application of simple logic. B's tend to appear more relaxed in the company of others and can take over or continue a task when A burns himself up.

Of course, not everybody fits the A or B categories — or at least they don't appear to from the outside. But it is worth asking yourself who — out of all of the people you know — tends to force the pace and winds up seeing their doctors for stress-related complaints. It is just possible that it could be you.

The study of life-events and their effect upon health has made it easier to understand why things that happen in our everyday lives can predispose us to both psychological and physical illness. What we now need to know is how the body handles stress and what happens to us in the process.

How the body handles stress

In biological terms, the origin of stress lies in survival. When primitive man had to hunt to stay alive, he faced the constant threat of being hunted himself, which meant standing and fighting or fleeing to escape death. This fight or flight response has been built into our mental and physical make-up and acts as a kind of computer programme which warns us of impending danger and prepares us for immediate action.

What actually happens to us when we mobilise ourselves for action is this: the brain receives a warning signal that alerts the hypothalamus, a nerve centre at the base of the brain. The pituitary gland — which is attached to the hypothalamus, releases an alarm hormone (ACTH) into the bloodstream which is conveyed to the adrenal glands which sit just above the kidneys. Stimulated by ACTH, the adrenal glands secrete adrenalin, noradrenalin, and cortisones which mobilise the body's defences and prepare it for 'fight' or 'flight'.

The autonomic nervous system constantly regulates the amount of energy we use up in coping with stresses of various kinds. It has two branches — the sympathetic and the parasympathetic which compensate for each other. The sympathetic nervous system speeds us up whereas the parasympathetic slows us down. When we are under stress, the sympathetic operates as a kind of advance guard, building up our strength in preparation for combat. The parasympathetic meanwhile acts as a calming mediator, controlling the release of energy.

In coming to terms with stress, adrenalin and noradrenalin act as an essential first line of defence, but their action is short-lived. Cortisol — the other hormone released by the adrenal glands — comes into play a few minutes after the initial stress-reaction has taken place and helps to stabilize the now stimulated organism. Its action is to bring up reinforcements by making sources of energy available from other parts of the body. This is done by increasing the production of sugar from stores in the liver; accelerating the breakdown of protein into animo-acids, which provides help in the repair of damaged tissue; mobilising fat or cholesterol for release into the blood and generally providing a protection against inflammation by the creation of scar tissue. Other reactions include an increase in the heart rate which pumps more blood — and hence more oxygen — to the muscles; the constriction of blood vessels in the skin and stomach enabling more blood supplies to be diverted to the brain; increased respiration as the lungs dilate to bring in more oxygen; contraction of the spleen to release more red blood corpuscles to help carry oxygen, and sweating — as the body temperature rises.

The picture you get from this description is of someone who is 'steamed up' and ready for action. The body is a superbly co-ordinated machine which generally protects itself from damage, however, prolonged over-stress can result in a breakdown of its compensatory mechanisms.

3 When the System Breaks Down

If we exhaust ourselves and then fail to take enough rest to compensate for the expenditure of energy, our bodies quickly begin to object. When we have enough sleep and rest we are much less likely to make ourselves ill. This is because the body's immune system deals with potentially harmful invaders by building up a system of defence — or immunity, against them.

It may well be that we are becoming less resistant to infection as we come to rely more upon externally-administered agents than our body's own natural self-regulating mechanism. When we become tired and run-down we probably don't realise that we are weakening our defences against infection. What happens is that our antibodies soon become overwhelmed by the invading antigens with the result that resistance fails and the body surrenders.

We have to produce new antibodies each time we are faced with a new threat in the form of a microbe or virus and it is when the battle to strengthen our protective devices is at its height that we experience most pain, inflammation and fever. Once the enemy is under control the healing process begins and the threat recedes.

When we are faced by a difficult emotional problem, the hypothalamus is aroused, which activates the pituitary gland — sending stress hormones to the adrenal glands which, themselves, secrete hormones called glucocorticoids. These inhibit the production of anti-bodies and consequently lowers resistance. This means that when you are under strain, you are more susceptible to illness than when life is calm.

Stress-related disorders

So, what kinds of threats to our health and well-being can we expect if we don't take proper care of ourselves? Well, all of us are different, and will respond differently to stress, but there is no doubt that at such times we all become more susceptible to simple things like colds and 'flu' and some of us become more accident-prone. At the more serious end of the scale, illness and disease may occur.

To some extent, susceptibility depends upon what kind of person you are. For example, outward-going, extrovert types may need to learn how to avoid becoming tense, so as to lower blood pressure and avoid putting strain on the heart. Inward-looking, introvert types may need to stop worrying in private to avoid anxiety and associated problems, like stomach disorders. There is also the question of emotions to consider.

Our bodies tend to reflect emotional ups and downs. Most of us have experienced nerves before an exam or interview when the stomach churns, the heart beats rapidly and the skin feels hot and sweaty. Grief, on the other hands, tends to slow the body down and drains away energy leaving us feeling tired and listless.

This means that stresses of various kinds — pleasurable or unpleasurable — alter the body's normal functioning in subtle ways and over a long period of time can actually upset the fine tuning.

Heart attacks are the biggest single killer of men in the Western World, and one wonders whether the pressure of modern life is not largely to blame. All kinds of factors have been identified as major causes of heart attacks — smoking, poor diet, lack of exercise, but only recently has stress been serious considered as a contender. A survey conducted by the now defunct Health Education Council in 1981, for example, found that members of the public regarded stress as the number one factor, whereas in a separate report, the Government rated it only number four behind the other risk factors mentioned above.

The aggressive type A person, that was referred to on page 39, is known to be more susceptible to heart attacks than the more placid type B person. But does this mean that such people are emotionally predisposed to heart disorders?

High blood pressure, or hypertension, occurs when the heart pumps blood under abnormally high pressure. Emotional factors are known to contribute to this condition and it is thought that like the coronary type a hypertensive may be an ambitious, though less confident individual.

Angina arises when too little oxygen reaches the heart, causing stabbing chest pains and a feeling of suffocation — it is thought to be more common amongst competitive though anxious types, whereas cardiac arrhythmia or 'heart flutters' tend to characterise people who are basically 'at conflict with themselves'.

Migraines, are caused by dilation of the blood vessels in the scalp and, may also have something to do with personality. The migraine sufferer is said 'not to know what to do with leisure' and tends to be rather insecure while at the same time wanting to be admired for his or her skills. When leisure is actually achieved, the migraine starts and with it a range of moods that contrast markedly with the normally controlled temperament.

Digestive disorders are also thought to result, in some cases, from stress. Upset stomachs, for example, are one of the most common complaints that doctors have to deal with.

Ulcers occur when the stomach is working overtime. People who get them are often competitive types who seem to live on nervous energy — with the result that they feel constantly on edge. Frustration, pent up anger, hostility, these are the kinds of emotional triggers that need to be identified in ulcer cases, because if they are allowed to continue for too long, illness can result.

Ulcerative Colitis occurs when portions of the large gut become so inflamed that bleeding and perforation take place. In milder forms, early treatment can remove the symptoms, but when the condition is serious, severe illness ensues, occasionally resulting in surgical removal of the colon. It has been suggested that a period of helplessness or despair can contribute towards ulcerative colitis and that people who find it difficult to show emotion are more prone to this kind of disorder.

One of the difficulties in proving that emotional stress is actually a cause of ill-health is that there is nearly always an alternative physical explanation. For example, diabetes occurs when there is insufficient insulin in the body cells to absorb glucose from sugar in the blood. Sugar provides energy but when, in the form of glucose, it is left unused, it merely accumulates in the blood. Getting rid of it, through urination is costly in terms of the demands it makes on water and salt. Meanwhile to make energy, the body has to burn fat instead, an inefficient method which results in other acids being released into the bloodstream further upsetting the chemical balance.

However, stressful situations are sometimes known to be associated with diabetes. Anger, reaction to danger and fear increase the sugar content in the blood, which if persistent, place such a strain on the pancreas — which is responsible for the production of insulin — that the system for metabolising glucose breaks down. On the other hand, diabetes can arise directly from pancreatic failure caused by physical stresses like infections, accidents and heart attacks. For this reason, it is always better to reserve judgement on possible causes until all the facts are known.

Emotional inflexibility can be a cause of stress and this may be why we reserve words like 'cold' or 'uptight' for people who have difficulty in showing their feelings or in relaxing. Relaxation is essential if you want to remain fit and healthy and therefore an inability to relax or let out emotion naturally can only store up stresses within the body. Most of us fail to realise that we actually prepare ourselves for pain or injury by ignoring the body's warning signals. Our muscles, for example, protect our joints by cushioning the impact of movement and if we weaken the muscles through lack of fitness, alcohol or tiredness, then we should expect to feel more aches and pains.

Muscles only require to be tensed when they are in use. If they continue tense after activity has ceased, then relaxation has not been accomplished. We find it increasingly difficult to relax due to both real and imaginary pressures. People tire easily and are more susceptible to aches and pains. Backache is notorious for causing time off work, not simply because hard physical exertion may be involved but because of reduced flexibility due to pressures of the job.

4 Taking the pain out of strain

Coping with stress rather depends upon how much control you have over the circumstances creating it. For example, environmental factors like noise, light and pollution probably lie beyond your control and therefore, coping relies to a large extent upon how well you adapt and whether you can minimise your contact with the stressors. Stresses associated with growth and development may, similarly, be difficult to handle because they are part of life.

Learning how to avoid situations or people that put you under strain is an essential first step in the direction of a more harmonious life. Changing your attitude to life can also go a long way towards improving your general outlook. For example, instead of charging headlong into a situation, sit back and reflect for a minute on the likely outcome — it might well be that you discover a simple route to solving the problem and one that demands less energy.

If you are someone who finds it difficult to motivate yourself and feels anxious about your lack of energy or drive, it is probably worth reflecting upon your purpose in life. It may be that you have never had to face a real challenge or are afraid of doing so. Perhaps the view you have of yourself is altogether too modest and it's time that you took a few risks in order to test your own abilities. This means looking to see if you have been capitalising upon your strengths rather than continually reflecting upon your weaknesses. Everybody has inhibitions, it's just that some people are better at covering them up than others. On the other hand, if you are a person who believes in the old adage of 'work before leisure' it may be worth asking yourself whether you have established the right balance between the two. It's all a question of finding one's optimum level of efficiency both at work and at play. The less effort you have to put into an activity the more likely you are to achieve your goal without frustration or strain.

Striking a proper balance between work and leisure is particularly important in reducing the effects of stress. One of the most obvious ways of ensuring that you get the best out of both worlds is to find a job that is satisfying and yet still allows you enough free time to relax. It is undoubtedly true that pleasurable work makes for more pleasurable leisure time. If you are out of work, it is still important to try to identify activities that interest you and to set yourself tasks each day just to preserve your sense of perspective. Self-respect quickly disappears when your livelihood is taken away, which is why hobbies and pastimes need to be kept up as far as possible.

Holidays are essential to health. Although some people claim that they never need time off, illness often forces them to stop and rest. A change of atmosphere and people is always a good thing to stimulate new thinking and re-adjust one's sense of perspective. Often, people realise how tired they have been only during the second week of a holiday when the pressure has finally lifted and it is not uncommon to hear people say that they were ill on holiday.

Leisure-time activities can be very therapeutic for people who don't know what to do with their spare time and find themselves getting depressed and anxious. Whether it's playing bowls, golf, joining clubs, or attending adult education classes, the practical use of free time plays an important part in counteracting frustration, apathy or the rigours of a day-time job. Keeping fit and healthy is one of the most important factors in stress-reduction and is an essential aspect of self-help. If you are unfit then your stress threshold will be lowered thereby increasing your susceptibility to ill-health. Jogging, tennis, squash, dancing — in fact any physical activity helps to tone up the body, relieve tension and provide breathing space.

Smoking is quite definitely a key factor in reducing all-over fitness. It really doesn't matter whether cigarettes make you feel better or seem to reduce tension, the fact is that they contribute to all kinds of illnesses and while you are unfit you are subject to greater pressure, which consequently makes you smoke more. The same kind of vicious circle exists with alcohol consumption. Wherever an intoxicant is used to compensate for feeling low, the long-term result is to produce greater stress.

Sleep plays a major part in regulating mood and maintaining health. Too little of it leaves you open to exhaustion and too much of it to lethargy. During deep sleep hormones are released which aid growth and replace dead cells which helps to even out the natural losses that occur in the course of waking activity.

A good sexual relationship can be one of the most effective and satisfying ways of relieving stress and tension. Sexual understanding is an important element in the business of coping with everyday life, because a good relationship provides a boost both to morale and to the sense of well-being that derives from it. Stress and tension have the effect of lowering sexual responsiveness and it is worthwhile remembering this if things start going wrong.

There are a large number of community-based, self help and support groups which exist to help people under stress. The 'Someone To Talk To' database, for example, holds over eight thousand addresses and telephone numbers of organisations throughout the United Kingdom, which work alongside the statutory health and social services provided by central and local government. A sample listing of helpful addresses is provided on page 69.

Professional help

By their nature, problems require solutions, and if these are not forthcoming, difficulties in coping can arise. This is particularly the case with mental and emotional problems. Depression, anxiety, phobia, hypochondria and psychosomatic illness usually require more than just a friendly chat and for this reason they tend to be presented to the already hard-pressed family doctor. General Practitioners treat nine out of ten cases of psychological disorder that present themselves during surgery hours. Only one in ten is referred to a psychiatrist. On top of all this the family doctor treats numerous other cases where psychological factors are suspected though the patients display only physical symptoms. Doctors are forced to make decisions quickly about people they often don't know, and rely to a large extent upon the prescription of drugs to deal with symptoms in the hope that these will disappear after a while. Many people worry about having to take pills and they have good reason to be concerned, because pills do not — in themselves — solve problems. However, *pharmacotherapy* — or treatment by use of drugs — is an extremely sophisticated method and should not be rejected out of hand. Tranquillisers, anti-depressants and sleeping pills can provide a much needed source of relief during periods of emotional disturbance or unhappiness.

Counsellors are sometimes to be found working alongside doctors although this practice is still relatively uncommon. They provide the important function of someone to talk to in a professional capacity — in much the same way that doctors used to counsel their patients. For someone who is nervous or anxious, has a marital or sexual problem or perhaps is suffering from a mild psychosomatic complaint, a counsellor can provide reassurance.

Psychologists, psychotherapists, psychiatrists and psychoanalysts are all trained to assess and treat psychological problems although, in general, minor stress-related complaints would not fall within their area of work. When someone displays signs of psychological disturbance — for example, a prolonged depression following the death of a wife or husband — then you might expect a referral to one of these professionals to take place.

Apart from the specialists there is also a range of professional and voluntary help available in the community to respond to individual need. Social Workers, health visitors, community nurses, lay clergy, volunteer workers and the advice and information-providing bodies like the Community Health Councils, the Citizens Advice Bureau — all combine to spread the net of support where it is most needed.

Holistic medicine

A criticism quite often levelled at conventional medical practice is that it fails to operate a genuinely preventive service, in that it concerns itself only with the management of ill-health. However, many people now accept the idea that the mind and the body are interrelated and that it is possible to participate more fully in the healing process.

In recent years we have witnessed the development of new approaches to health often referred to under the title of 'holistic medicine'. Originally branded as 'alternative medicine', because of its supposed antagonism towards traditional medical practice, a more open-minded attitude seems to be emerging amongst practitioners on both sides.

The terminology used to describe the various disciplines within the holistic field is, however, still a little confusing.

Complementary medicine for example, means finding the right combination of therapies to bring the individual back to full health (i.e. to complement to make whole). This is perhaps one reason why the term 'holistic' is used, because it looks at the individual's physical, mental, emotional and spiritual health as part of the whole being.

The *natural therapies*, which can generally be interpreted to mean acupuncture, osteopathy, chiropractic, homeopathy, naturopathy, herbalism, reflexology and healing, form part of holistic (or if you prefer, complementary medicine.

Acupuncture

Acupuncture originated in China and is a technique involving the insertion of special needles in carefully selected sites around the body which correspond to certain organs or body functions. The Chinese believe that health means being in harmony with the elements and energies of the natural environment (Yin and Yang), therefore treatment of any kind of disorder is essentially aimed at restoring this harmony. Acupuncture is widely accepted as a treatment for the relief of pain and discomfort and is known to relieve the symptoms of many disorders including asthma, migraine, backache, ulcers and emotional stress.

Osteopathy

Osteopathy is a manipulative technique used not only in the treatment of mechanical disorders of the spine, but also in the relief of symptoms of ill-health brought about by a lack of alignment between the joints, muscles and nerve-endings. Through the release of natural energies within the vasular, nervous and lymphatic systems, the body is returned to a state of harmony. Although it is not widely appreciated, osteopathic techniques can prove equally effective in the relief of psychosomatic and stress-related illnesses.

Chiropractic

Chiropractic is also a manipulative technique. The main difference between chiropractic and osteopathy lies in the way in which manipulation is practised. Osteopathy tends to use leverage and massage, whereas chiropractic relies more upon the application of direct pressure upon the joint in question. Once again this technique is effective in the treatment of a wide variety of disorders because mechanical realignment automatically relieves pressure upon the central nervous system.

Medical practitioners are able to refer patients to osteopaths and chiropractors providing that overall responsibility is retained by the doctor.

Homeopathy

Homeopathy works on the principle that a substance when given to a healthy person produces certain symptoms. Minute quantities of the same substance can be given to alleviate conditions showing the same symptoms.

Naturopathy

Naturopathy is an approach to illness which emphasises the importance of the natural healing forces already present in the body and views symptoms of disease as a manifestation on the part of the body attempting to heal itself. In this sense it is a radical departure from orthodox medicine which views the suppression of symptoms as an essential first step to cure. A naturopath is more of a teacher than a doctor, because his aim is to advise his patients on how best to help themselves by altering their lifestyles in beneficial ways. By emphasising the links between mind, body and behaviour, naturopathy teaches that balance can restore health to the diseased organism. It works particularly well for acute conditions of the digestive and bronchial systems.

Herbalism
Herbalism is a very ancient system of medicine which relies upon plants and their extracts to prevent and cure disease. The best known English authority on this subject was probably Nicholas Culpeper, whose major study of herbal remedies was first published in 1653.

After taking a complete medical history, the herbalist will tailor-make a treatment to suit your body rather than the disease, this way, a greater emphasis is placed upon your own self healing abilities.

Many modern drugs are based on traditional herbal remedies. For instance, the willow bark has for years been used to alleviate pain, whilst its modern counterpart is known as aspirin.

Reflexology
Reflexology is a relation of acupuncture, but relies instead on pin-point pressure on the soles of the feet or hands to re-establish the harmony of those organs directly influenced by these pressure points.

Healing

Healing is something that all holistic practitioners are engaged in, however there are some who have particular abilities to generate the vitality or life-force required by the sick person. The way this is done varies according to the philosophy of the individual healer, although there is one rule common to all bona fide practitioners, which is that healing should be offered with the thought that the patient's needs come before the simple eradication of symptoms. In this way the patient is allowed to return to health at a pace which he or she can accept.

The natural therapies mentioned above are a selection of the better established systems of holistic medicine. Many other techniques exist, some more reliable and well proven than others. For further information about holistic approaches within British Medical Practice, contact the British Holistic Medical Association, 179 Gloucester Place, London, NW1 6DX (Tel: 01-262 5299), or for information about the scope of holistic medicine and training standards for practitioners, contact the Institute for Complementary Medicine, 21 Portland Place, London, W1N 3AF (Tel: 01-636 9543).

5 Stress-reducing techniques

For most people, coping with stress is a matter of finding some kind of outlet. Strain tends to occur when stress builds up and cannot be usefully channelled into some kind of activity. There are all kinds of ways of ensuring that a happy medium is achieved, most notably thought stress-reduction techniques like yoga, meditation, autogenic training, biofeedback, relaxation methods and lifeskills training.

Yoga
Yoga is part of the Hindu religious philosophy that emphasises the merging of the human spirit with the 'universal spirit' and in the West has found its most popular expression in Hatha yoga — a system

of postures and breathing exercises that bring relief from stress and help to improve mental and physical health.

Yoga classes are run by a variety of organisations and it is worth checking at your Town Hall or library to see if there are any being run in your area. Although yoga exercises look rather uncomfortable they are in fact designed to increase mobility and suppleness of the body. Mental concentration combined with correct physical posture ensures that strain is avoided and research has shown that during Hatha relaxation exercises, blood pressure and blood cholesterol levels can be significantly reduced.

Meditation

Like yoga, meditation has its origins in the East. It aims to achieve a higher state of consciousness than that experienced in the everyday world, by means of an inward-looking thought process that concentrates upon the 'oneness' of the self and the body. There are many kinds of meditation — as there are yoga methods — and it is worth reading up on them before selecting the one you wish to practise. Transcendental Meditation, for example, is a fairly simple, though effective technique that can be practised both at work and at home.

Inner-awareness is brought about through the focussing of attention upon a *mantra* — a word or series of words, or a *mandala* — visual forms, both of which one repeats or reproduces in the imagination.

These induce a state of calm and well-being whereby external influences are effectively shut out. Meditating in this way brings peace to both mind and body and results in feelings of warmth and relaxation.

There is no doubt that meditation is a useful technique for reducing stress. It has been found that during meditation, the heart-rate slows, oxygen consumption is reduced and brain-waves assume a characteristic 'alpha pattern' which is associated with complete relaxation and sleep.

Autogenic Training
This is a form of Western meditation which comprises a set of exercises that you use to develop a state known as passive concentration — where you are fully conscious of achieving a state of peace while completely relaxed. By concentrating on parts of the body becoming 'heavy' or 'warm' it is possible to achieve a pleasurable sense of calm and well-being.

The general aim of autogenic training is to enable you to understand and control both mental and physical processes more effectively, so that you are free of strain and less subject to ill-health. It has been shown to be just as effective in dealing with stomach ulcers as it has in helping people to lose weight.

Further information about autogenic training and stress reduction techniques can be obtained from the Positive Health Centre, 101 Harley Street, London W1. Tel 01-935 1811.

Biofeedback

Yoga, meditation and autogenic training are very helpful if you are not already so anxious that you find it difficult to relax in the first place. Biofeedback may be more appropriate for people who find it difficult to relax because it provides a means of changing your own reactions in response to electrically-monitored readings of your bodily functions.

It is difficult under normal circumstances to control involuntary processes like heart rate, blood pressure, sweating and brain waves and yet yogis have consistently proved that it is perfectly possible to do so. Until recently, people in the West have not been able to reproduce the same kind of experience, however, biofeedback machines have now been developed to enable us to monitor these bodily processes and to find ways of controlling them.

Stress is known to reduce the amount of alpha-wave activity in the brain — electrical waves associated with relaxed states of awareness. Therefore, it stands to reason that learning how to control the underlying processes that result in reduced alpha-wave activity, will help to create greater relaxation.

Biofeedback, basically works like this: a machine monitors electrical activity through pads attached to various parts of the body — for example, muscles in the case of cramps. As the body records activity due to tension, it causes a flood of electricity which produces a tone in a pair of earphones. The more you are able to relax, the quieter the noise in the headphones becomes, until in a state of complete calm, you experience silence.

Alpha-wave training has been shown to be particularly helpful for migraine and high blood pressure sufferers and tension headaches caused by stress respond very well to this technique. Biofeedback machines can be obtained relatively easily and cheaply although before you decide to invest in one, it might be worth consulting your doctor first.

Relaxation Methods

The main aim of relaxation is to gain voluntary control over physical and emotional processes so that strain can be avoided. This requires recognition in the first instance that you are not relaxing properly and then a self-disciplined approach towards understanding how the mind and body interact in strain, pain and ill-health.

Relaxation teaching provides instruction on posture, control of muscular tension and breathing, as well as a range of techniques for reducing discomfort such as massage and physical exercises to increase mobility. Mastering such techniques can help towards resolving the kinds of problems that people face when they are tense, nervous and under strain, like persistent headaches, migraines and insomnia. Learning how to relax also makes it easier to cope with traumatic life-events such as bereavement and demanding situations like childbirth, and has also been shown to have beneficial results for women who suffer from pre-menstrual tension.

Lifeskills training
Lifeskills refers to a series of methods developed by the British Psychologist, Dr Robert Sharpe, which involves the use of tape cassettes dealing with practical issues like relaxation skills, over-coming shyness, coping with exams, giving up smoking and controlling one's weight.

It is reasonable to assume that during our lives we learn to develop bad as well as good habits. Lifeskills training aims to help people to overcome problems by re-learning patterns of behaviour. The techniques are not simply directed towards relaxation because sometimes in order to overcome certain stresses, assertiveness needs to be emphasised.

The behavioural approach to stress management may not suit everybody but it is certainly a practical approach and can provide help for problems ranging from fatigue and phobias to sexual difficulties, and insomnia. Further information and cassettes can be obtained from Lifeskills, 3 Brighton Road, London N2 8JU. (Tel: 01-580 4972).

Coping with stress is a personal matter until it becomes too much to handle. Strain and distress often result in others becoming involved. The British attitude of 'keeping a stiff upper lip' may seem admirable, but there is little to be gained from covering up tension or worries.

This book has attempted to cast a general eye over the subject of stress and how it motivates or over-stretches us. It cannot provide answers to peoples' individual problems, but it does explain how you can help yourself to recognise the effects of stress and strain and it suggests a number of ways of coping when the pressure becomes too great. If, as a result of reading this book, you have discovered any new things about yourself or about the way you lead your life, then it will have served its purpose.

Some useful books

UNDERSTANDING STRESS AND ANXIETY by C. Speilberger published by Harper and Row, 1979.

STRESS AND RELAXATION by Jane Madders published by Martin Dunitz, 1981.

REAL HEALTH by Alex Poteliakhoff & Malcolm Carruthers published by Davis Poynter, 1981.

THRIVE ON STRESS by Dr Robert Sharpe and David Lewis published by Souvenir Press, 1977.

STRESS by Walter McQuade and Ann Aikman published by Hutchinson, 1976.

'STRESS' — HUMAN BEHAVIOUR SERIES by Ogden Tanner published by Time-Life Books, 1976.

STRESSFUL LIFE EVENTS — THEIR NATURE AND EFFECTS by B.S. and B.P. Dohrenwend published by John Wiley & Sons, 1977.

LIVING WITH STRESS published by Consumers Association Publications, 1982.
A GUIDE TO ALTERNATIVE MEDICINE by Robert Eagle, BBC Publications, 1980.
THE STRESS OF LIFE by Hans Selye published by Longmans, 1957.
ALTERNATIVE MEDICINE by Andrew Stanway published by Penguin Books, 1982.

Useful addresses

The information provided below has been made available by the *Someone To Talk To* Database Project.

For further information please contact:
Dr Dick Thompson
Someone To Talk To Project
8 Hallam Street
London W1N 6DH Tel: 01-636 2985 / 6 / 7

Ageing

Age Concern
Bernard Sunley House
60 Pitcairn Road
Mitcham
Surrey CR4 3LL
Tel: 01-640 5431

A national network of local groups serving the needs of the elderly.

Association of Carers
21-23 New Road
Chatham
Kent ME4 6QJ
Tel: 0634 813981 / 2

A support network for those caring for others.

National Council of Carers and their Elderly Dependents
29 Chilworth Mews
London W2 3RG
Tel: 01-724 7776

A support network for those caring for the elderly.

Alzheimer's Disease Society
Bank Buildings
Fulham Broadway
London SW6 1EP

Tel: 01-381 3177

Network of support groups offering help to families.

Alcohol Problems

ACCEPT
200 Seagrave Road
London SW6 1RQ
Tel: 01-381 3157

Help, advice and self help groups service for those with alcohol problems.

Turning Point
4th Floor
CAP House
9/12 Long Lane
London WC1A 9HA
Tel: 01-606 3947 / 9

The leading service provider in the field of drug and alcohol misuse, operating residential and non residential projects.

Alcohol Concern
305 Grays Inn Roaad
London WC1X 8QF
Tel: 01-833 3471

National agency on alcohol misuse which can provide a list of established regional councils on alcoholism within the UK.

Asthma

Asthma Research Council (Head Office)
St Thomas's Hospital
Lambeth Palace Road
London SW1 7EH
Tel: 01-226 2260

Support to asthmatics and their families, so that they understand and control their condition. Promotes research. 90 local branches.

Birth Control and Abortion

British Pregnancy Advisory Service (Head Office)
Austy Manor
Wootton Wawen
Solihull
West Midlands
B95 6BX
Tel: 05642-3225

Brook Advisory Centre (Head Office)
Walworth Centre
153a East Street
London SE17 2SD
Tel: 01-703 1234 / 1390

International Planned Parenthood Federation
17-20 Regent Street

London SW1
Tel: 01-235 7576

A full family planning information across countries and religions.

Family Planning Association
27-35 Mortimer Street
London W1N 7RJ
Tel: 01-636 7866

A professional training and education service on all aspects of personal relationships and sex education.

Cancer

Cancerlink (Head Office)
46a Pentonville Road
London N1 9ME
Tel: 01-833 2451

Gives information about Cancer treatments and forms of support.

B.A.C.U.P. (British Association of Cancer United Patients)
121 / 123 Chaterhouse Street
London EC1M 6AA
Tel: 01-608 1661

Provides information to help cancer patients, emotional support and practical advice.

Counselling

British Association for Counselling (Head Office)
37a Sheep Street
Rugby
Warwickshire CV21 3BX
Tel: 0788 78328

National body providing information about counselling services and individual counsellors.

AIDS

Terrence Higgings Trust
PO Box No. BM AIDS
London WC1N 3XX
Tel: 01-242 1010

National organisation providing advice and information on acquired immune deficiency syndrome.

Sexual Problems

Albany Trust Counselling
24 Chester Square
London SW1 9HS
Tel: 01-730 5871

A personal counselling service for individuals and couples with all types of sexual identity and relationship problems.

Bereavement

CRUSE (Head Office)
Cruse House
126 Sheen Road
Richmond
Surrey
TW9 1UR
Tel: 01-940 4818 / 9047

Counselling and practical advice for the widowed and their families.

Still Birth and Neonatal Death Association

Head Office
Argyle House
29-31 Euston Road
London NW1 2SD
Tel: 01-833 2851

Offers help, advice and information .

Depression

Fellowship of Depressives Anonymous
36 Chestnut Avenue
Beverly
Humberside HU17 9QU

Tel: 0482 860619

Network of support groups for sufferers from depression.

Manic Depression Fellowship
51 Sheen Road
Richmond
Surrey TW9 1YG
Tel: 01-940 6235

An organisation of self-help groups for manic depressives, their relatives and friends.

Samaritans
17 Uxbridge Road
Slough
Berkshire SL1 1SN
Tel: 0753 32713 (Head Office)

A 24-hour confidential service to help the suicidal and despairing. The telephone number of your local branch will be in the phone book.

Diabetes

National Diabetes Foundation
177a Tennison Road
London SE25 5NF
Tel: 01-656 5467

Supports diabetics with information and the development of local groups.

Drug Problems

Turning Point
CAP House
9 / 12 Long Lane
London EC1A 9HA
Tel: 01-606 3947

An organisation offering advice, rehabilitation and care to alcohol and drug abusers, their families and friends.

Release
169 Commercial Street
London E1 6BW
Tel: 01-377 5905

Rehabilitation and care for drug abusers.

Tranx
17 Peel Road
Harrow
Middlesex HA3 7QX
Tel: 01-427 2065

Support for those taking long-term prescriptions and tranquillisers.

Gambling

Gamblers Anonymous
17-23 Cheyne Walk
London SW10

Tel: 01-352 3060

Help, advice and information.

Holistic Medicine

British Holistic Medical Association
179 Gloucester Place
London NW1 6DX
Tel: 01-262 5299

Council for Complementary & Alternative Medicine
Suite One
19a Cavendish Square
London W1M 9AD
Tel: 01-409 1440

Council of professional bodies representing acupuncture, chiropractic, homeopathy, medical herbalism, naturopathy and osteopathy.

Institute for Complementary Medicine
21 Portland Place
Westminster
London W1N 3AF
Tel: 01-636 9543

Central agency providing information on natural therapies and complementary medicine.

Koestler Foundation
10 Belgrave Square
London SW1X 8PH

Tel: 01-235 4912

Information and advisory service on all aspects of health self-care and alternative/complementary medicine.

Positive Health Centre
101 Harley Street
London W1
Tel: 01-935 1811

Autogenic training courses for stress management.

Incest and Child Abuse

Incest Crisis Line (Head Office)
32 Newbury Close
Northolt
Middlesex UB5 4FJ
Tel: 01-422 5100

National HQ for network of telephone counsellors dealing with all aspects of child sexual abuse within the family.

Loneliness

Nexus
Nexus House
Blackstock Road
London N4 2JE
Tel: 01-359 7656 / 6073

Provides the opportunity to communicate on many different levels with other single people.

Marriage and Friendship Counselling Club
25 Kings Road
London SE3 4RP
Tel: 01-730 5142

An organisation to help find new friends.

Solo Clubs for the Divorced, Widowed and Separated
Room 7 / 8
Ruskin Chambers
191 Corporation Street
Birmingham
West Midlands
BR4 6RY
Tel: 021-236 2879

Organises friendship groups.

Marriage and Divorce

Divorce Conciliation and Advisory Service
38 Ebury Street
London SW1
Tel: 01-730 2422

A service to help those wanting and involved in divorce.

Organisation for Parents Under Stress (OPUS)
106 Godstone Road

Whyteleafe
Surrey CR3 OEB
Tel: 01-645 0505

Help and advice to parents who may harm their children.

National Marriage Guidance Council
Herbert Gray College
Little Church Street
Rugby
Warks CV21 3AP
Tel: 0788 73241

Maternity Advice

Miscarriage Association (Head Office)
18 Stoneybrook Close
West Bretton
Wakefield
West Yorkshire WF4 4TP
Tel: 092-485 515

Contact for details of 80 local groups. Information and support to women and families during and after a miscarriage.

National Childbirth Trust
9 Queensborough Terrace
London W2 3TB
Tel: 01-221 3833

Contact this address for local groups. Antenatal teaching, breastfeeding counselling, postnatal support.

Post Partum Depression
44 Ferncroft Avenue
London NW3
Tel: 01-435 6976

Help and advice for mothers suffering from post partum depression and for their families.

Association for Post-Natal Illness
Queen Charlotte's Maternity Hospital
Goldhawk Road
London W6 OX9
Tel: 01-748 4666

Help and support for those with post-natal depression.

Mental Health

Mental Health Foundation
8 Hallam Street
London W1N 6DH
Tel: 01-580 0145 / 6

Britain's leading grant-making charity in the mental health field.

MIND (National Association for Mental Health)
22 Harley Street

London W1N 2ED
Tel: 01-637 0741

Provides legal information, training and educations advice to people with mental health problems and their families.

Migraine

British Migraine Association
178a High Road
Byfleet
Weybridge
Surrey KT14 7ED
Tel: 09323 52468

Information, understanding, funds volunteers for research into migraine, leaflets/newsletter free to members.

Migraine Trust
45 Great Ormond Street
London WC1N 3HD
Tel: 01-278 2676

Advice, counselling, information and free literature for migraine sufferers and their relatives.

Psychological Problems

Association for Group and Individual Psychotherapy
29 St Marks Crescent

London NW1 7TU
Tel: 01-485 9141

A central organisation for group and individual psychotherapy.

British Association of Psychotherapists.
121 Hendon Lane
London N3 3PR
01-346 1747

Clinical service in psychotherapy for individual adults and children.

London Clinic of Psychoanalysis
The Institute of Psychoanalysis
63 New Cavandish Street
London W1M 7RD
Tel: 01-580 4952 / 3 / 4

National Organisation to give low-cost psychoanalysis to those who cannot afford private treatment.

Retirement

Pre-retirement Association of Great Britain and Northern Ireland
19 Undine Street
London SW17 8PP
Tel: 01-767 3225

Support and help for those who are going to retire or are retired.

Smoking

ASH (Action on smoking and Health)
5-11 Mortimer Street
London W1N 7RH
Tel: 01-637 9843

Information on how to give up smoking and lists of local support groups.

Stress

International Stress & Tension Control Society
The Priory Hospital
Priory Lane
Rohampton
London SW15 5JJ

An organisation providing lectures and conferences on stress

Lifeskills
3 Brighton Road
London N2 8JU
Tel: 01-580 4972

Mail-order self help cassettes to control stress.

Positive Health Centre
101 Harley Street
London W1
Tel: 01-935 1811

Autogenic Training courses for stress management.

Stress Syndrome Foundation
Cedar House
Yalding
Maidstone
Kent ME18 6JD
Tel: 0622 814431

Provides training courses in stress management, leaflets and information on al aspects of stress.

Yoga for Health Foundation
Ickwell Bury
Northill
Biggleswade
Bedfordshire
SG18 9EF
Tel: 0767 27271

National organisation with local clubs and centres throughout Britain.

Women's Health Information

Women's Health Information Centre
52-54 Featherstone Street
London EC1Y 8RT
Tel: 01-251 6580

Library on women's health, national register of women's health groups and self-help groups.